Enchanting SPAIN

JOHN MacDONALD & PATRICIA DÍAZ PEREDA

JOHN BEAUFOY PUBLISHING

Contents

Above: The fairy-tale fortress in Segovia.

Above centre: Torimbia Beach in northern Spain.

Above left: One of the typical restaurants of Castile and Léon.

Opposite: Casa Batlló in Barcelona, designed by Gaudí, was built in 1877.

Title page: The Jewish Quarter, Córdoba, with the Great Mosque in the background.

Chapter 1: Spain, Just a Little Different

'Every country and society is different, but Spain is a bit more different', so Julian Pitt-Rivers, the acclaimed British anthropologist, is supposed to have said. But what defines Spain as a nation?

Popular culture and tourist expectations would suggest flamenco and bullfighting as prime candidates. Flamenco is certainly part of Spanish culture, it is still evolving with contemporary versions of the performance being well received. Bullfighting, of course, is iconic but it is losing ground in some areas and banned in Catalonia though still an established part of Spain's heritage and culture. Probably the best-known bullring is at Ronda in Andalucía, which is regarded as the home of modern bullfighting.

If, however, we look deeper and consider the influences that have shaped Spain then we must take account of the Roman occupation. Not only is there an architectural legacy both artistic and utilitarian but perhaps the Romans' most important gift was language. Other major cultural influences include Jewish and Arabic; the latter having stamped its mark on almost all Spain and most firmly in Southern Spain.

Spain's post-Franco democracy is based on the 'Constitution of 1978', which established the framework for the present system. The parliamentary monarchy has the monarch as head of state with the prime minister taking the title of 'President of the Government'. The Spanish parliament, or Cortes Generales, is bicameral and composed of a lower house, the Congress of Deputies, and an upper house, the Senate. The deputies are elected by universal suffrage approximately every four years. The role of first minister is performed by the president, while the monarch acts as head of state. There is, however, a very strong republican movement in Spain supported by parties from both sides of the political divide.

Spain itself is divided into 17 autonomous communities and two autonomous cities, Ceuta and Melilla, Spain´s North African enclaves. The communities themselves are

further divided in 50 provinces. The autonomous regions each have a President and Council of Ministers, allowing for genuine decentralization. The importance of the provinces has declined somewhat since the introduction of the autonomous communities during the immediate post-Franco era, they still, however, form the electoral districts for national elections. The provinces were the foundation of the autonomous communities and therefore no province exists in more than one community.

The tourist industry, dubbed the 'Spanish Miracle' by some observers, is a success story that grew from the tempestuous post-Civil War years. In the top five most visited countries for 2014, the population more than doubles during the August high season. Tourism, encompassing the Spanish climate, gastronomy and culture as well as the sheer exuberance for life is a commodity relished by those from the colder, greyer lands of northern Europe.

Added to these, the sheer diversity of the Spanish landscape is breathtaking. Fertile plains such as that in Castile in the north and the Vega of Granada in Andalucía are in sharp contrast to arid Almería or the wonderful and dramatic landscape of the Guadix area. The mountains which separate the coastal plains from the hinterland also separated the peoples of Spain, establishing regional differences and strengthening the diversity of the people. These barriers were only penetrable with donkey and pack before the advent of Spain's modern road system.

It is now a joy to drive on Spain's excellent motorway system and the surprises that the landscape throws up are remarkable. Even on the flattest plain a crag is likely to appear as surreal as any Dalí painting. The geography of the country is an ever-changing pageant of mountains, plains, colours, textures and shapes. It never ceases to delight or inspire.

Opposite above: The bullring at Ronda.

Above: Cabo de Gata, southern Spain.

Opposite below: A traditional Flamenco dancer.

Geography and Climate

Spain has a falling population of 46,507,760 as of the 1 January 2014, some 17 million fewer than the UK but with over twice the land area. It is the second largest country in western Europe behind France, its 504,645 sq km (194,844 sq miles) total landmass is divided into 17 autonomous regions including the Canary and Balearic Islands.

One geographical fact which takes many visitors by surprise is Spain's altitude. Averaging 660 m (2,165 ft) above sea level, it is the second most mountainous country in Europe matched only by Switzerland. The Spanish capital, Madrid, is the highest major European capital and also the third largest in terms of population and metropolitan area.

Spain is country of plateaus (*mesetas*) and mountain ranges. The Central Meseta, covering some 250,000 sq km (96,526 sq miles) is by far the largest and the major element in defining the topography of the country. The plateau is the heartland of Spain, the mysterious 'Plain of Castile' that romantically 'lay before' erstwhile travellers.

and with a vengeance after rains or with thawing snow. Many impressive bridges both modern and ancient span wide ravines where one would expect to find deep and expansive watercourses, but which, however, usually only show a gentle flowing stream or empty gully. There are exceptions, of course, and Spain has five major rivers, four of which, the Duero, Tajo, Guadalquivir and Guadiana flow into the Atlantic, while the Ebro empties into the Mediterranean.

Summer temperatures can be punishing. In 1994 a temperature of 47.2°C (116.9°F) was recorded in Murcía. Average summer temperatures for Málaga, as an example, are a very pleasant 25°C (77°F) while in January and December they average 13°C (55.4°F), northern Spain's averages are some five degrees lower. In February 1956 at Lake Estangento, Lleida, a temperature of -32°C (-25.6°F) was recorded. Average yearly rainfall for the whole country was 636 mm (25 in) in 2014. But averages don't tell the whole story and extremes occur. The southern Tabernas Desert has just 200 mm (8 in) per year, whereas the fertile northern autonomous community of Galicia is drenched with over 1,000 mm (39 in).

Its seemingly endless horizon, altitude and dryness of air combine to produce wonderful sunsets and a superb quality of light generally.

The two highest mountain ranges are the Pyrenees to the north, forming the border with France, and the Sierra Nevada of Andalucía, whose precipitous, rocky northern face and gentle, rolling, southern slopes are quite distinctive. The highest point in continental Spain is Mulhacén in the Sierra Nevada at 3,478 m (11,411 ft).

Other major ranges in the north are the Picos de Europa, the highest peak being Torre Cerredo at 2,648 m (8,688 ft), the Cantabrian Mountains and the strategically important Sierra de Guadarrama, which slices diagonally through the Central Meseta, and to the south, the Sierra Morena with Bañuela its highest point at an elevation of 1,332 m (4,370 ft).

Spain is not a country of rivers. Most of the 1,800 rivers are virtually dry during the summer months but flood quickly

Opposite: The Sierra Guadarrama, north of Madrid.

Above left: The Picos de Europa in northern Spain.

Above: Bridge over the River Tajo at Almaraz, Cáceres province.

Flora and Fauna: The Spanish Garden

Of Europe's 9,000 plant species some 8,000 thrive in Spain. Altitude, climatic conditions and soil quality cause a great diversity in the flora of the country, which ranges from the Alpine species of the high sierras in the north to the succulents found in the semi-deserts of Almería.

Oak forests and rolling green landscapes give way to plant life adapted for the more arid regions, cork and evergreen oak, cacti and palm trees. Perhaps the two plants which are arguably most representative of Spain are the bougainvillea and the olive tree. Bougainvillea along with adelfas and oleander can be seen around balconies, down the central reservation of motorways and in hedges, with colours so bright they hurt the eyes. The olive tree is extremely important to Andalucía and Spain as a whole with over 2.4 million ha (5,930,529 acres) given over to its cultivation, making Spain the world's largest producer of olive oil. The trees stretch over the landscape following the natural profile of the land, they grow on the plains and cling to the sides of crags, they cover hilltops and grow in the depth of valleys. Every commercial tree in Andalucía is tracked by the Junta de Andalucía (Regional Government) and each has a GPS reference, such is their importance.

The animal life of Spain is an amalgamation of European and African species. On the Bay of Biscay coast, whales and dolphins bask and romp, while on the Mediterranean shore monk seals sun themselves on the sandy beaches. Wolves and the Brown Bear still prowl the central and northern regions, while the Spanish Lynx, once almost extinct, has been bred in captivity and released into the wild. Over 300 now wander the arid Andalucían landscape. Other mammals include the Spanish Ibex, red deer and otter. The

African influence can be seen from the Egyptian Mongoose, chameleon and Common Genet, Iberia being the only region of Europe where the genet occurs. Reptiles are represented with over 20 lizard species and 30 snakes, of which almost half are venomous.

One of the joys of travelling in Spain is the bird life, eagles still soar over the fields and hills in search of prey and Spain is the home to the world's largest population of Black Vultures. When in central areas, particularly Castilla La Mancha, the White Stork, which breeds on the Iberian Peninsula and winters in central and southern Africa, is an amazing sight. These untidy birds build their huge, untidy nests on high-tech masts, chimneys and belfries but for some unexplained reason they seem to favour the roofs of churches. They look incongruous in the parched landscape being so far from sources of water.

The plant and animal life of Spain seems exotic to those from the cooler climates of northern Europe, the rich mixture of European and African species is just another example of the unique charm of Spain.

Above: The White Stork is a traditional bringer of good fortune and offspring.

Right: Bougainvillea, an iconic plant of Spain.

Opposite left: A mild climate and fresh water coming from the Sierra Nevada contribute to the fertility of land in Andalucía.

Opposite right: The introduction of breeding groups of Spanish Ibex into the wild has achieved a rising population, which will hopefully save the remaining two subspecies from extinction.

A Potted History

It has been said that Spain is a confluence of two continents and two seas. It could be described as a crossroads between Europe and Africa and a bridge between the Atlantic and Mediterranean. These circumstances help to make Spanish history complex, full of passion and very turbulent.

From Pre-history to the Visigoths

Evidence from the Sierra de Atapuerca in north-eastern Spain suggests that human habitation dates back at least 780,000 years. In 1879 a wonderful sequence of pre-historic paintings were discovered in the Altamira cave of northern Spain. The cave is widely known as the Sistine Chapel of pre-historic art. Images of deer, horse and bison in superb detail and colour give us a tantalizing glimpse into the world of the ancients.

During the Bronze Age, Celts from across the Pyrenees and Iberians from North Africa mixed with the local population, the result was the emergence of the 'Hispani' people. During this period the Mediterranean was a highway of trade. Spain became an integral part of this commerce through the Iberian state of Tartessos. Situated between the lower reaches of the Guadalquivir and Guadiana Rivers, it was a place of myths and legends. The Phoenicians founded the city of Gadir to give them a base on the Peninsula from which to exploit this commerce. Gadir, now known as

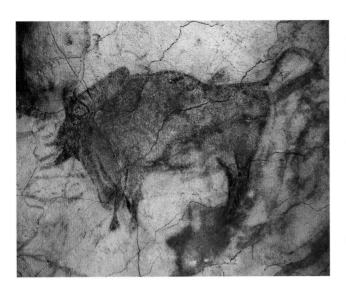

Cádiz, is possibly the oldest continuously occupied city in the western world.

The Romans invested heavily in Spain; it took them almost 200 years to subdue the unruly inhabitants. The hero Viriatus led a spirited resistance before being betrayed and killed in 139 BC. There were in fact two Roman provinces on the Peninsula: to the north Hispania Citerior with Tarraco, modern-day Tarragona as its capital and Hispania Ulterior to the south, with Córdoba its principle city. The Romans occupied the Iberian Peninsula for some 700 years and Latin began its passage towards the Spanish language of today.

As the Roman Empire contracted, so the Vandals and then the Visigoths from the north put in unwelcome appearances. Known mainly for their sacking of Rome, they also pillaged the western Mediterranean with great alacrity. The Vandals certainly lived up to their name in terms of destruction but it was they who first attempted to unify Spain.

The Moors

A highly suspect story involving King Roderick, the last of the Goths, maintains he forced his attentions upon the unfortunate daughter of a particularly vengeful count. This, so the story says, prompted the Moorish invasion of Spain. Whatever the truth is, in 711 AD Muslims from North Africa entered the Peninsula and drove the Visigoths from their stronghold of Toledo. With them they brought a new culture, and new ideas in art and architecture, which have left their mark on Spain to this day and caused Spain to develop very differently from the rest of Europe.

Above: Painting of a bison on the ceiling of the Altamira cave.

Right: The Roman arena at Mérida.

Opposite: The inlaid tile recess at the Plaza de España, Seville, depicting the province of Cádiz.

In 756 AD Muslims fleeing Syria established the Umayyad dynasty and Córdoba went from strength to strength, soon becoming one of the most populous and successful cities of the age. However, infighting among the various Muslim factions kept them relatively weak militarily. This inherent weakness eventually let to the first Christian victory by Don Pelayo at the battle of Covadonga, one of the first stirrings of the 'Christian Reconquest' of Spain. This gathered pace and in 1085 Toledo fell to Alfonso VI. Nine years later Rodrigo Díaz de Vivar, better known as El Cid, took Valencia. During the momentous year of 1492, the last of the Moors were driven out of Granada by Isabella and Ferdinand.

Above: A typical, Arabic-style courtyard in the Alhambra, Granada.

The Golden Age

Now that the costly war of reconquest was complete, funds were available to finance Columbus's voyage of discovery, something Columbus had been petitioning for since 1486. It was the wise Isabella who convinced the sceptical Ferdinand to sponsor the expedition. What followed fundamentally changed the course of history as the New World revealed its enormity and potential.

The 16th and 17th centuries were both momentous and disastrous. Spain flourished in the arts during their 'Siglo de Oro' or Golden Age. Under the Hapsburg King Philip II, the Empire expanded at an unprecedented rate. Exploration in the New World extended Spanish influence and brought an influx of wealth. However, as the Empire grew, so the conditions which would ultimately cause its decline were being put in place. Demographic, political and social problems coupled with military overstretch soon emptied the coffers. The monarchy declared bankruptcy on four separate occasions. Influence started to wane with wars, unrest and corruption hastening the process.

During the reign of Philip II the 'Black Legend' began to spread throughout Europe. This was a body of literature that vilified the King and the Spanish people, depicting them as brutal, bloodthirsty fanatics. Spain's enemies, religious, military and economic, were interested in perpetuating the Legend out of jealousy for Spain's empire, which was the largest ever known. The Legend exaggerated the excesses of the Inquisition and the conquest of the Americas, yet in the rest of Europe institutionalized cruelty and the burning of witches were the norm. The Black Legend has had a negative effect on the collective psyche of the Spanish people.

The French Occupation

Spain's support for France during the early years of the Napoleonic War eventually led to the French occupation of Spain and in 1808 Napoleon Bonaparte's brother,

Joseph-Napoléon Bonaparte, took the Spanish throne. Napoleon, however, underestimated the will of the people, who rose in revolt. The 2nd May 1808 is a date that resonates throughout Spain's recent history. Immortalized by Goya's paintings, it marked the popular uprising which led to the Spanish War of Independence. This conflict, known in the English-speaking world as the Peninsular War, was pivotal in the defeat of Napoleon. Without the Spanish guerillas causing havoc among the French troops, Wellington could never have landed at Lisbon and the outcome of the Napoleonic War could have been very different. 'Pepe Botella' became Joseph Bonaparte's Spanish epithet due to his fondness for a drink.

1814 to 1874 were turbulent years. Ferdinand VII was on the throne but his reign was less than auspicious. Colony after colony was lost in the New World and his ultraconservative, anti-liberal stance soon brought conflict. A series of civil wars broke out, first against Spanish liberals, then the republicans. After his death in 1833, a struggle for the throne followed between the moderate Queen Isabella and her uncle, the Infante Carlos. These were the destructive Carlist Wars, but even after these conflicts the mayhem continued with revolutions against the discredited Isabella. It wasn't until 1874, when the popular Alfonso XII took the throne, that some semblance of stability was achieved. Despite this, turmoil continued with the loss of Cuba and the Philippines as a result of the Spanish-American conflict of 1898.

1923 brought a military coup that installed Miguel Primo de Rivera as dictator. His elitist thinking and ability to alienate lost him the support of the monarchy, intellectuals and those who might be expected to underpin his authority. When the military turned their back, he fled to Paris. Alfonso XIII, who had initially supported Rivera, lost popularity and tested opinion by calling provincial elections. Republican candidates were returned in the vast majority of provincial capitals; Alfonso abdicated and also headed for Paris. Signatories to the Pact of San Sebastián in 1930 formed a provisional government.

The Second Spanish Republic

In 1931 the Second Spanish Republic was proclaimed. The Republic brought agrarian reform, votes for women, secular schools and obligatory education. The years from 1931 to 1936 saw three changes of government. Political loyalties swung from the left to the right and back again, laws were put on the statute books, repealed and passed again. Land-owners backed by the military cynically disregarded land reforms and brutally repressed those who demanded their rights. In 1936 Generals José Sanjurjo, Emilio Mola and Fransisco Franco launched a failed coup attempt, which led to three years of calamitous civil war. Britain, France and the United States refused to support the legitimate government of Spain, while Hitler's Germany and Mussolini's Italy supported Franco's Nationalists. Only Mexico and the Soviet Union supported the Spanish Republic. As Mexico had limited resources, so Russia had a hidden agenda.

One of the most cynical acts carried out during the conflict was the bombing of the Basque city of Guernica. At the behest of Franco, aircraft of Hitler's Condor Legion and the Italian Aviazione Legionaria bombed the town on 26 April 1937 targeting for the first time a civilian population, a precursor to Hitler's blitzes of the Second World War. The outrage at Guernica was made famous by Picasso's painting *El Guernica* but other cities also suffered extensive air attacks. In March 1938 Barcelona was bombed by Italian aircraft from the Balearic islands, the attack lasted three terrible days. Madrid was attacked constantly during the conflict and its residential areas dive-bombed for five full days. This destruction earned Madrid the title of 'The Crucified City'.

Without the help of the western democracies the outcome was inevitable and with the defeat of the Second Spanish Republic, 36 years of the Franco dictatorship followed. Spain emerged a democratic nation after the death of Franco in 1975 with European Union membership following in 1986.

Culture: The Spanish Identity

Spain's contribution in the fields of art, architecture and literature through individual genius has been profound. In science, too, eminent Spaniards have produced ground-breaking work of universal importance.

Architecture and Art

Architecture in Spain has always been outstanding from the first settlers through to the 21st century. The names of the masters of the Roman style may be lost to us forever but their architecture remains in central and northern Spain; the south being dominated by *arte andalusí*, as a result of the original Muslim dominance. In the 12th century the *mudéjar* style appeared, which was a fusion of Christian and Muslim forms. The Gothic period (12th–15th century) was followed by the architectural movement so closely linked in Spain with Diego de Siloé (1495–1563), the architect and sculptor who designed Granada Cathedral. Another important advocate of Renaissance architecture in Spain is Juan de Herrera (1530–1597), designer of the Monastery of El Escorial, completed in his typical austere style. José de Churriguera (1665–1725), an architect and sculptor, created masterpieces in the Baroque style, while Juan de Villanueva (1739–1811) designed the magnificent Prado Museum building. Antoni Gaudí, perhaps one of the best-known Spanish architects worked during the 19th and 20th centuries producing wonderfully idiosyncratic edifices (see pages 42–43). The last decades of the Franco dictatorship saw architecture shining again, through people such as Sainz de Oiza, but it was only in the 1990s that Spanish architects won high international prestige. The list of internationally acclaimed Spanish architects is a long one but Rafael Moneo (1937) is worthy of special mention, winning the Pritzker Prize for Architecture in 1996 and the RIBA Royal Gold Medal in 2003.

From Altamira´s cave paintings (approximately 18,000 years ago) to Picasso (1881–1973), artists with palette and brush have thrived in Spain. El Greco (1541–1614), although born in Crete, found inspiration during the Spanish Renaissance. During Spain's magnificent Golden Age Velázquez (1599–1660) rose above all others, influencing Manet, Picasso, Dalí and Francis Bacon. His contemporaries included names such as Murillo, Zurbarán and Ribera. Goya's (1746–1828) individual style is regarded as the precursor of the 20th century avant-garde movements. Juan Gris (1887–1927) and Picasso, as well as the Frenchman Braque, created Cubism. And no mention of Spanish painters would be complete without the eccentric Catalan, Salvador Dalí (1904–1989), who excelled in surrealism.

Left: The brick-and-stone-built Church of Santiago de la Luz is considered one of the best examples of 'mudéjar' art in Toledo.

Opposite: Casa Garrido, Madrid.

Below: The Dalí Theatre and Museum in Figueres, Catalonia.

Literature

Spanish literature is among the richest and most vivid in the Western world. In 1492 Nebrija wrote a Spanish grammar, the first for any of the Romance languages. The Spanish poets who excel are so numerous we must cherry pick and start with the Renaissance and the 'Gentleman Soldier' Garcilaso de la Vega (1499–1536). Next a priest, Fray Luis de León (1527–1591), who was teaching at the Salamanca University when he was arrested and imprisoned by the Inquisition. Released five years later, he simply continued the lesson from the point it was so rudely interrupted with the words, "as we said yesterday". Other names include the mystic poet San Juan de la Cruz (1542–1591) and Santa Teresa de Jesús, poet and writer.

The picaresque novel is a wonderfully Spanish invention. The genre involves episodic tales with a low-born scallywag of a hero, who lives on his wits in an unjust society. The first picaresque novel was *El Lazarillo de Tormes* written by an anonymous author and dating from at least 1554. The style has been widely imitated in England, France and Russia. The genre evolved to become more pessimistic, sarcastic and the humour more critical. One of the most important novels after this evolution was *El Buscón* by the poet and novelist Quevedo (1580–1645) writing during the Golden Age (see page 12).

The Golden Age lasted more than 150 years around the middle of 16th and 17th centuries. The most important author was Cervantes (1547–1616) with his masterpiece *Don Quijote de la Mancha* and its two immortal characters, Don Quijote and Sancho Panza. Known worldwide, it is one of the most translated books ever. Of the other names, the poet and playwright Lope de Vega (1562-1635), Góngora (1561–1627), probably the most original and influential poet of the Golden Age, Quevedo (already mentioned) and the playwright Calderón de la Barca (1600–1681) are the most important.

The Romanticism movement saw poets and writers such as Rosalía de Castro and Gustavo Adolfo Bécquer among others.

Realism was also an important movement in Spain and writers such as Benito Pérez Galdós (1843–1920) excelled. According to some critics he is the most important Spanish novelist since Cervantes.

The 'Generation of 98', so named after Spain's loss of its last colony, Cuba, in 1898 produced very important writers such as the novelist Pío Baroja (1872–1956), the thinker and novelist Unamuno (1864–1936), the playwright and novelist Valle Inclán (1866–1936) and the poet Antonio Machado (1875–1939). The Generation of 98 was succeeded by such literary greats as the poet Juan Ramón Jiménez (1881-1956), who won the Nobel Prize in 1956.

The 'Generation of 27' (sometimes called the Silver Age in comparison with the Golden Age) reached its peak during the Second Republic and the Spanish Civil War (1936–1939). The group of Generation of 27 poets included Federico García Lorca (1898–1936), Pedro Salinas (1891–1951), Luis Cernuda (1902–1963), Rafael Alberti (1902–1999) and Vicente Aleixandre (1898-1984) who won the Nobel Prize in 1977. After the war, most of these went into exile, Lorca was murdered by Nationalists at the start of the War and the poet Miguel Hernández (1910–1942) died in jail.

Science

Spain has contributed to the sciences especially in the field of medicine. Miguel Servet's (1509/11–1553) greatest achievement was the discovery of the blood circulation in the lungs. However, Servet was eventually arrested and burnt as a heretic in Geneva.

Santiago Ramón y Cajal (1852–1934) received the Nobel Prize in Medicine. He was one of the first to investigate the microscopic structure of the brain and became known as the 'Father of Modern Neuroscience'. Other important doctors were Gregorio Marañón (1887–1960), Severo Ochoa (1905–1993), a Nobel Prize winner, biochemists Margarita Salas (b. 1938) and Mariano Barbacid (b. 1949), anthropologist Juan Luis Arsuaga (b. 1954), physicist Álvaro de Rújula (b. 1944), the quantum physicist Juan Ignacio Cirac (b. 1965), and Pedro Cavadas (b. 1965), an internationally renowned doctor specializing in limb transplants. Not to forget mechanical engineering and Juan de la Cierva (1895–1936), the inventor of the 'autogiro', precursor of the helicopter, and Isaac Peral, inventor of the submarine.

These are but a few of the individuals who have shaped Spanish culture and benefited mankind as a whole.

Left: Don Quixote and Sancho Panza statue in the Plaza de España, Madrid.

Opposite: One of the highlights of the Dalí Museum is the Mae West Room.

Gastronomy: The Spanish Stomach

En el sur se fríe, en el centro se asa, en el norte se guisa. 'Frying in the south, roasting in the centre and in the north, stews': a Spanish view of their own cuisine. Perhaps broadly true but by no means the whole story. Stews are, of course, universal and originated from ordinary people trying to make the best of the ingredients they had to hand. Certainly the *fabada Asturiana* is from northern Spain, traditionally Asturias, as the name would suggest. It's a bean stew and gets its name from the *fabes la Granxa*, a type of white runner bean. It's a hot and heavy winter dish eaten across Spain.

The *cocido Madrileño* is a singular, chickpea-based stew from Madrid that crosses all social boundaries. The origins of the dish are lost in the mist of past centuries, however the Sephardic kosher dish *adafina*, created in the Middle Ages, is one of the possible precursors. It was extremely popular in Spain a hundred or so years ago when it became a national dish. The most costly ingredient was the meat, which varied in quality and quantity depending on the pocket of the diner. The *estofado* could be called the generic Spanish stew. Based on beef, veal, chicken or rabbit and made with paprika and water rather than stock, it is eaten all over the Spanish-speaking world.

Frying in the south: a wild generalization perhaps but the Spanish certainly fry. Dishes include *croquetas*, which can be made of chicken, ham or seafood, sausages and many kinds of fish, usually cooked very simply – just salted and floured. *Puntillitas* are particularly popular, these are deep-fried, whole baby squid. *Patatas a lo pobre*, potatoes and onions slowly fried in olive oil with plenty of salt, are simple, cheap and wonderful. *A la plancha* is a frying technique where a small amount of oil is used and the pan or griddle is allowed to get very hot prior to cooking. Salmon, chicken or pork cooked in this way is succulent and wholesome. The wonderful egg, potato and onion *tortilla* or Spanish omelette is another masterpiece of Spanish cooking; every household and restaurant claims its own secret recipe.

Opposite right: *Alioli (mayonnaise with garlic).*

Opposite left: *Fabada Asturiana.*

Above: *Sardines grilling on the night of San Juan, Santiago de Compostela.*

Top: *Paella de Valencia.*

The *asados* or roasts of Castile are traditionally *cochinillo asado* (suckling pig) and *cordero* (suckling lamb), which are cooked with water and white wine, while roasted vegetables are a familiar dish throughout Spain.

There are, of course, foods that don't fall into any of the three categories, such as *paella*, a rice-based dish, which is not fried but traditionally cooked over an open fire. The Valencian seafood version is eaten all over Spain and is familiar to most. *Gazpacho* and its thicker cousin *salmorejo* defy categorization, perhaps cold soups could describe them, but they are certainly delicious and so well suited to the summer heat.

Food is seasonal, as it is in most countries. Spanish-grown fruit and vegetables are of exceptional quality, as is the acorn-reared pork and the marbled beef. Fish is very important in the Spanish diet and, along with Japan, Spain has the highest consumption worldwide.

Tapas

Tapas are made by a whole range of cooking methods. The word 'tapa' translates as 'top' or perhaps 'cover' and is thought to derive from the habit of putting thin slices of bread or ham on top of wine glasses to stop impurities from falling in or itinerant insects from helping themselves. In some areas of Spain they are known as *pinchos*. They are now small plates of food accompanying a drink. The variety of tapas available is only limited by imagination. A tradition has built up around the consumption of tapas and has led to the phrase 'ir de tapas' (going out for tapas). It involves going from bar to bar and sampling the different tapas on offer, this is usually done while standing at the bar, presumably gravitational pull helps in the digestive process, it is also less formal, which is what this style of eating is all about. Tapas competitions are common and some cities have 'the week of the tapa' where internationally renowned chefs compete with their own sophisticated versions. In Fuengirola they have an annual erotic tapas competition which isn't for the faint-hearted.

Desserts

Only to be found in summer is the *horchata*, typical of Valencia, a delicious drink made from tigernuts that also can be taken as a dessert. Those who have a sweet tooth will find an amazing variety of cakes, rolls (*bollos*) and desserts. Among the traditional desserts are *arroz con leche* (a form of rice pudding) from Asturias, *natillas* (egg custards) from Castilla, fritters and flans (*crème caramel*). The *torrija*, typically from Madrid and Castilla, consists of bread soaked in milk, dipped in egg batter and fried in very hot olive oil, then covered with sugar and cinnamon. Other desserts include Catalonian custard and *tocinos de cielo*, both quite sweet.

The first written mention of marzipan (*mazapán*) appears in *The Thousand and One Nights* and several countries claim its invention. In Spain, it is said that the nuns of the

Convent of San Clemente in Toledo invented the confection when the city was suffering famine after the Battle of Navas de Tolosa (1212) and the only foods available were almonds and sugar. In the instructions for the confectioners of La Mancha written in the 17th century, it states that the almonds must come from Valencia and the sugar must be white, it also added honey and eggs to the recipe.

In Spanish homes weekday meals are usually finished with fruit, sweet deserts are more for Sundays or for when eating out at a restaurant. The traditional *merienda* (afternoon tea) in Madrid would be drinking chocolate with *churros* (sweet fried dough) but as the areas of Spain are so diverse, so are the deserts with some only eaten on feast-days.

Wine and Cheese

Wine is a must to accompany any food and Spain has a great diversity from the medium-bodied Rioja, known throughout the world, to the crisp, dry, white wine produced from the Verdejo grape. But try wine from the smaller vineyards or the local *vino de la tierra*, it is surprisingly good and offers great value for money. Bread, wine and cheese are a wonderful combination with Spain having more than 200 cheese varieties.

Spanish food and wine are a delight waiting to be sampled, you only have to be in Spain with an appetite. No matter what method of cooking is used, olive oil is always the oil of choice, of which Spain is the largest producer in the world. From north to south, from east to west, Spanish gastronomy is one of diversity, dishes from the most simple to the most sophisticated place Spanish cuisine as one of the best in the world.

Left: *A traditional grape harvest.*

Above left: *A small selection of Spanish cheeses.*

Opposite top: *Nowadays, marzipan is only eaten at Christmas, except in Toledo where one can enjoy it all year round.*

Opposite below: *'Horchata' and 'fartons' (donut-like pastries) for afternoon tea.*

Ferias and Festivals: The Zest for Life

Finding a *feria* (a local festival) in Spain is simple, in fact they are so numerous it seems they find you, finding the stamina to see one through, however, is the difficult part of the exercise. There is a certain spontaneity about these kinds of events in Spain. Even though they are in general well organized, they go off at tangents, they steer their own course irrespective of planning.

On the night of San Juan (23 June), it is traditional to jump over bonfires to ward off evil spirits. One enterprising individual in Santiago de Compostela, Galicia, tired of waiting his turn, was seen to start his own small bonfire over which to leap. This promptly inspired others to do the same and the plaza soon became a danger to public safety. Another particular *feria* in Fuengirola, Andalucía, was due to start on the Saturday but as everything was in place on the Thursday, it was just too much of an effort for it not to start. These first two 'illicit' days were said to be the best of the carnival as the forces of law and order were caught on the hop and the event went unpoliced much to the delight of the more adventurous participants.

Whether the celebration is religious or simply a carnival, sometimes this distinction is rather grey, they are always well attended and supported with a passion that only the Spanish can muster.

Religious Festivals

Easter week is celebrated with the Semana Santa (Holy Week) processions over the whole of Spain. Málaga in Andalucía sees over 40 individual processions each corresponding to a particular brotherhood identified by the colours of their robes and tall *capirotes* (hats). The *tronos* (floats or thrones) carried in procession can weigh more than 5,000 kg (5½ tons) and are moved with a swinging motion by dozens of bearers. The floats, each depicting part of the Easter narrative, are welcomed with applause and tears, such is the strength of feeling they evoke. Even if you don't share the same religious beliefs, you cannot fail to be moved by the piety and emotion of those crowding the procession's route. These events attract tens of thousands, so if you haven't booked a seat at the procession's destination, then it is advisable to view them from their church of origin. The local tourist office can supply itineraries.

All towns have Christmas festivals, particularly on 5 January, the day before *El Dia de Reyes* (Three King's Day). This is a children's favourite as the venerable trio dispense sweets as their procession passes. Corpus Christi is another important date (eight weeks after Easter) involving processions, religious observances and feasting. In Toledo, 70 km (43 miles) south of Madrid, preparations begin a month before the actual day. In the Plaza Zocodover virtually every window displays textiles embroidered with crests, coats-of-arms and Eucharistic symbols. The procession takes three hours to make its way via the Plaza Zocodover to the Cathedral and includes representatives from all spheres of society. The young girls dressed in white for their first communion are particularly enchanting.

Spanish towns have *ferias* for all occasions as well as at least one celebrating the community under the auspices of the local Virgin. These can last seven or more days and start late morning with noisy processions that continue towards dawn and beyond. One requires stamina and a basic understanding of how to survive in such a heated and intense environment. Each *peña* (club or group of like-minded people) offers entertainment ranging from traditional flamenco to renderings from Broadway shows. Fuengirola's main *feria* takes place during October when the evenings are cooler and demonstrates that the Spanish zest for life isn't dampened by thoughts of the approaching winter.

Opposite: The Fuengirola Fair, the Feria del Rosario'.

Above: The Semana Santa or Easter Week processions are a time of piety and observance. Many of the brotherhoods wear the traditional pointed 'capirote'.

La Mercè Festival

Barcelona's main *feria* is the La Mercè Festival which takes place around 24 September. Usually a five-day event, it is held in honour of Mare de Deu de la Mercè, the Patron Saint of Barcelona. One of the highlights is the fire run (*correfoc*) along the Via Laietana where fire-breathing dragons spray the crowd with incendiary sparks and 'devils' throw fireworks. This may sound alarming but it is really quite safe as long some simple precautions are taken. In the Plaça de Jaume Human Towers (*castellers*) are built and a Giants' Parade (*gigantes*) takes place.

Las Fallas

Giants also feature in the Valencian festival of Las Fallas, which takes place during March. The *fallas* are papier-mâché statues often six metres (20 ft) tall, which are displayed all over the city. Some satirize politicians and television stars while others depict fantasy images. It's not just giants on offer during Las Fallas, every day at 2pm an event called la Mascleta occurs in the Plaza del Ayuntamiento. This involves rival areas or barrios competing with fireworks to make the loudest explosion. The event culminates with *masclets* exploding simultaneously. Not for those of a nervous disposition, the sight and sound of massed pyrotechnics detonating can be unnerving. Towards the end of the festival the *fallas* are burnt at midnight during the *Nit del Foc* (Night of Fire).

The Night of San Juan

The night of San Juan (St John) not only involves the exorcising of evil spirits but also welcomes the summer. The sardine harvest is at its peak and they are at their best. Charcoal fires spring up in almost every plaza and the tantalizing aroma of fried sardines pervades every street and doorway. In many cities the sardines are offered free of charge and their consumption is accompanied by music and dancing.

Food is very important to the Spanish and an important part of any *feria* or festival. Local seasonal fare is always available to delight and recharge the flagging festival-goer. Dedicated food fairs cater for the more discerning or adventurous but no matter what event you attend, there is never a shortage and the diversity is staggering.

Opposite left: *Casteller at La Mercè Festival, Barcelona.*

Above: *Running of the bulls at the San Fermín Feria, Pamplona.*

Opposite right: *'Las Fallas Festival', Valencia.*

The Running of the Bulls

No mention of Spanish festivals would be complete without the mention of the Spanish Fighting Bull (*Toro Bravo*). The bullfight or *corrida de toros* is well known and regarded as a cultural event with fight reports appearing alongside theatre critiques in the country's newspapers. The Running of the Bulls, which involves risking life and limb while trying to outpace a herd of rampaging bovines, is a popular event across Spain. The most widely known, *El Encierro*, takes place during the Fiesta of San Fermín in Pamplona, Navarra, between 7 and 14 July. Participants run the 825 m (2,707 ft) from the bull's corral in Calle Santo Domingo to the bullring, preferably ahead of the bulls. The run usually lasts three to four minutes but it has been known to take ten if the bulls aren't feeling particularly cooperative. One favourite at these events was *El Ratón* (The Mouse), a 500-kg (1,100-lb) bull who acquired instant fame after goring a spectator to death during the Sagunto festival. His total tally was three killed and 30 injured. El Ratón fetched huge fees for appearances and assumed cult status before his death in 2013.

Arts and Crafts

Craft industries in Spain have been showing something of a rival over recent years with Andalucía leading the way in intricate wooden furniture, ceramics and leather goods. Other more traditional craft industries are facing increased competition from imported goods, especially from China.

Opposite page: *Toledo is world-renowned for the craft of 'damasquinado' and pieces using this technique make wonderful gifts.*

Below: *Manufacturing a 'Jarapa' rug in Pampaneira, La Alpujarra.*

The *tallers* (studios) of many craftshops in Spain are open to the public where you can watch traditional art and craft items being made. Buying from the workshop is a pleasing experience as you know your piece is authentic, and the charm of watching it being made by an artisan using the processes of bygone days is an added bonus.

Hand-made Rugs

In La Alpujarra behind the southern slopes of the Sierra Nevada there is a tradition of manufacturing *jarapas*, hand-made rugs using recycled fabrics. They are made on hand-operated looms using bold colours in a loose and coarse weave, and are hardwearing and easy underfoot. In the village of Pampaneira it is possible to watch the slow, painstaking process taking place as the carpet is woven on centuries-old looms. It is advisable to make any purchase from the workshop as many of the more touristy shops in the village sell reproductions from the Far East.

Esparto

Esparto grows in many countries but the Spanish grass is recognized as being of the highest quality. It is woven into rugs, baskets and rope to name but a few of its uses. The craft of esparto is spread across Spain with the Almería area being particularly active. If you are buying an esparto gift, why not a pair of traditional Spanish espadrilles – *alpargatas de esparto* – comfortable, strong and admirably suited to the hot summer months. Volunteers for the International Brigades during the Spanish Civil War donned *alpargatas* in favour of hobnailed army boots during their crossing of the Pyrenees.

Leather goods

Andalucía historically was the heart of the Spanish leather goods industry, and in particular Ubrique and the surrounding towns. Much is owed to the local Cork Oaks and the high-quality vegetable tannins they produce, which are needed to process the leather. Latterly, however, over half of Spanish leather tanning takes place in Catalonia, Valencia, Murcia and Madrid. During the Muslim occupation of Andalucía leather-working techniques were introduced from North Africa and the Spanish noun for leather work, *marroquinería*, is derived from the word Morocco. During the Middle Ages Córdoba became the centre of excellence for leather embossing; high-quality products (belts, purses, wallets, travel bags, etc.) are now available all over the regions of Cádiz, Córdoba and Granada. Equestrian leather goods are another Andalucían tradition with saddles and saddlebags much in demand while gun cases, chaps and game totes are ever popular. No reference to Spanish leather goods would be complete without a mention of the town of Valverde del Camino, where superb riding boots are manufactured. Enter any shop selling leather goods in Spain and the nostrils are assailed by that wonderful, ancient and yet familiar aroma of new leather, which seems to guarantee quality. It is said that the stronger the aroma, the more likely the leather is to be Moroccan and not Spanish.

Metalwork

Further north the metalworking of Toledo is remarkable and world-renowned, from swords and knives to delicate gold inlaid boxes of every conceivable size. The technique for

inserting gold or silver thread into etched metal to produce designs and text is known as *damasquinado*. The quality of Toledo steel is legendary; during the 16th and 17th centuries swords manufactured in the City fetched premium prices.

In Granada wood and bone inlay or *taracea* is a local craft learnt during the Arab occupation of Spain and originating from Syria and Egypt. The wood and bone are coordinated and combined to form borders and geometric patterns on boxes, wooden wall panels and trays. These pieces are wonderfully made and eye-catching as well as not being overly expensive, making them a popular souvenir.

Ceramics

Hand-made ceramics although common throughout Spain tend to be localized to towns such as Nijar in Almería Province and La Rambla in the Province of Córdoba, the east of Spain also specializes in ceramic tiles. Design and glaze differ from region to region but sadly many small workshops are closing with the younger generation unwilling to continue family businesses. One of the most interesting ceramic pieces, a speciality of La Rambla, is the intricate lampshade. Designed in Arabic style they adorn many local hostelries in the area. Not really a practical buy for the visitor, however, as they are rather too heavy for the meagre baggage allowance of most airlines.

Sports and Lifestyle

The Spanish lifestyle is a gregarious one. Human contact, physical and verbal is important, complete strangers will engage you in conversion anywhere and anytime. Mature ladies will poke you with their fans (*abanicos*) to stress some point or other and men will clasp you tightly by the shoulder; it isn't a subdued ritual either, for the Spanish to talk in whispers is an act of great self-control.

During the heat of a summer afternoon a Spanish home with have its blinds dropped and awnings lowered, the doors will be closed and air-conditioning units whirring. The siesta will be taken, then the only people on the streets will be tourists and those unlucky enough to be working. It will be in the cool of the evening when the squares, terraces and parks throng with life and pre-dinner drinks are taken with friends; the rhythm of life is continuous and pulsating. Dinner is usually eaten around ten at night, while lunch can be taken as late as three after a lengthy aperitif, and

merienda, afternoon tea, at five fills the gap for those who take it. Desayuno or breakfast served up to eleven is another social occasion. To adjust from the normal northern European eating times to the Spanish is something akin to jet-lag and requires a similar amount of time to readjust.

Being an outdoor people, sport is very important to the Spanish. Football dominates and their successes are greeted with a euphoria, which demonstrates their passion for the game but confounds the forces of law and order, who usually simply block streets and leave them to their celebrations. The rivalry between Real Madrid and Barcelona is worthy of note, it is fierce, partisan and emotional, the game on the field reflects the politics off it. In a taberna in Granada the question was asked why no one

cheered when Barcelona scored, the reply was "Because we are Spanish".

Motorcycling is immensely popular, in the world of Moto GP, the Spanish currently have four of the top five riders in the world. Tennis, of course, is also widely followed and played in Spain. The country has produced many fine players, not least Rafael 'Rafa' Nadal, considered one of the finest clay-court players in history.

Opposite: The Estadio Santiago Bernabéu in Madrid is the home of Real Madrid football club. Opened in 1947, it has a capacity of over 85,000.

Above: MotoGP is an extremely popular sport in Spain. The Jerez Circuit at Jerez de la Frontera is the national venue for the sport.

Chapter 2: Northern Spain

This is 'Green Spain', where the rainfall is plentiful and the landscape is one of rolling hills, dramatic mountain ranges and wild beaches. Stretching from the Atlantic to the Mediterranean, it is a region of diversity, not only with the ever-changing countryside but also the people. The summer temperatures are mild and the region attracts those who want to wallow in the art and culture of northern Spain, such as the architecture of Bilbao and Barcelona, laid-back San Sebastián or the friendly folk of Santiago de Compostela.

Galicia and Santiago de Compostela

Capital of Galicia in north-western Spain, Santiago de Compostela is a place of pilgrimage being the final destination on the Way of St James. People travel here from points all over Europe. In 2010, which was a 'Holy Compostelan Year', when 25 July falls on a Sunday, more than a quarter of a million people made the journey. The hospitality of the Galician people is staggering, pilgrims and tourists are welcomed with a genuine warmth. The Galician language is relatively widely spoken in Santiago with almost 25% speaking nothing else, while the vast majority of people are bilingual. Santiago de Compostela is also a university city alive with the ambience of the young and the studious.

A 'must-see' is the traditional Abastos morning market. All kind of fresh products are available including Galician seafood recognized as being among the best in the world. You can buy seafood here and take it to a restaurant in the market, where they will prepare it for you.

Above: The west façade of the Cathedral viewed from Obradoiro Square. A church was erected after the grave of St James the apostle was discovered in the city. It was, however, destroyed by Muslims in 1075. Work then began on a new cathedral in the Romanesque style. The most able craftsmen worked on the project including Master Mateo who, among other things, designed the outstanding 'Pórtico de la Gloria'. The west part including the main entrance is considered one of the most important and beautiful Romanesque monuments of the world. The Plaza de Obradoiro is the monumental centre of Santiago de Compostela and probably took its name from the Galician word meaning 'workshop' mainly because of the masons working on the cathedral. This and the buildings around it form part of the Old Town, now a UNESCO World Heritage Site.

Below: The university college, Fonseca, was built in the 16th century for Archbishop Alonso de Fonseca, in the house of his birth. The first seat of the University was founded under the sponsorship of his family. Nowadays the palace houses the General Library of the University with more than 300,000 volumes.

Left: The old, the young, Christian believers or those walking the route just for the experience, they all come. Identified by the ubiquitous scallop shell, they arrive foot-sore, but jubilant. It is a hard journey, the average is 20–25 km (12–16 miles) per day, some, however, prefer to be on bicycles or horseback. The scallop shell has always been the symbol of the pilgrims making their way to Santiago de Compostela. The origin is the miracle of the 'Gentleman of the Scallops'. A boat in danger was seen by a wedding group while they were walking on the beach. The groom went to help but a giant wave took him and his horse to the depths of the ocean. He asked God for help and he and his horse were brought safely to the beach, covered by scallops, at the same time as a boat bringing the corpse of St James from Palestine arrived at the shore. The miracle of their survival was promptly attributed to the deceased apostle.

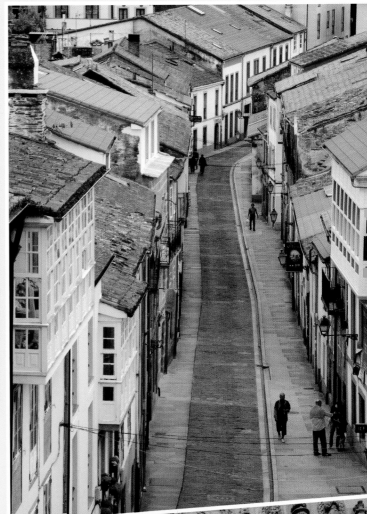

Above: The east façade of the cathedral, Quintana Square and the Gate of Forgiveness. The clock tower (also known as Berenguela) has a massive base but becomes more elegant as it rises. The clock has only one hand and due to a fault in the mechanism sometimes strikes thirteen, when this happens it is said that the devil walks abroad during the extra hour.

Right: Detail of the façade of the Hostal of the Catholic Kings in the Plaza de Obradoiro featuring the 12 apostles. Built as a resting place for pilgrims some 500 years ago, it has been described as the oldest hotel in the world.

.

Above right: A characteristic of Galician architecture is the use of a 'galería', a wooden structure with windows attached to the façade that gives the house very efficient protection against humidity but also allows daylight in. This probably started in the 18th and is still used widely in the 21st century.

Asturias and the Picos de Europa

Covering an area of 10,604 sq km (4,094 sq miles), Asturias on the Mar Cantabrico (Bay of Biscay) coast is one of the northernmost provinces. Asturias is a land of lush meadows, high rugged mountains, hidden coves and untamed beaches. Agriculture thrives due to the fertility of the land and the province supplies the vast bulk of the country's dairy needs. Known for its cheeses, especially the blue Cabrales and the soft 'Queso de Afuega'l pitu', Asturias has been called 'The Land of Cheeses' due to the diversity and quality of the product. Asturias is separated from the province of León by the Cantabrian mountain range of which the 'Picos de Europa' (Peaks of Europe) is part.

Above right: 'La Ruta del Cares' is one of the most spectacular walking routes in Spain and probably in the whole of Europe. The route is about 11 km (7 miles) long between the villages of Caín and Poncebos. The path is carved out of the rock of the mountains and crosses a gorge (nicknamed 'The Divine Gorge') over the River Cares. It's not too difficult if you're fit, but whatever your fitness level, it is worth the effort to complete even part of the route.

Right: The Naranjo de Bulnes (2,519 m/8,264 ft)) is one the most emblematic peaks in the Picos de Europa and legendary for Spanish climbers with the first ascent being made in the summer of 1904. In good weather the peak's silhouette is unmistakable. Some say the Picos were so named because they were the first land sighted by ships returning from the Americas. Whatever the truth, the range is truly spectacular where glacial conditions have created an area of remarkable alpine karst. The mountain range encompasses three massifs and has an area of 550 sq km (212 sq m). It has many high peaks with more than 250 over 2,000 m (6,560 ft), 40 higher than 2,500 m (8202 ft) and 14 over 2,600 m (8,530 ft) It was declared a National Park in 1918 and was the first protected area of the country.

Above: Enol Lake in Covadonga Park, north-west of the Picos, lies at 1,000 m (3,280 ft) above sea level and is the largest of three glacial lakes, one of which is only full of water during the spring thaw.

Right: The coast is only half an hour's drive from the Picos de Europa. Torimbia Beach is one of many wild beaches which are wondrous places in winter as well as summer.

Left: The indigenous Asturcón pony, which is black during the summer but turns brown as its winter coat grows is one of the oldest and purest breeds of ponies in the world dating back to 80 BC.

Centre: These traditional 'hórreos' are wooden barns to protect stored produce against humidity and animals. They are mainly used for corn, vegetables, fruit and pig products. One surprising characteristic of their design is their portability. They can be moved from place to place as necessary due to their screwless construction.

Below far left: Awarded Denominación de Origen, 'cabrales' is a cheese traditionally made by cattle farmers with cow's milk or a mixture of cow's, sheep's and goat's milk (all fed on mountain pastures). Ripening takes place in natural caves and lasts between two and four months. Originally made for local consumption, it is now marketed commercially. Asturias has 42 traditional cheese varieties.

Left: Asturias was the first cider-producing region of Spain and the drink has been made here since before the Roman invasion. The image shows the method of pouring the golden fluid. The cider is poured against the side of the glass from a substantial height. One then takes a swallow but not too much. Some has to be left in the glass so it can be cleaned (with the cider), as the glass is shared, hopefully only between family and friends.

Navarra and the Basque Country

Navarra shares a 163-km (101-mile) stretch of border with France. Its capital, Pamplona, is famous for the 'Running of the Bulls' (see page 25). The provinces of Álava, Biscay and Gipuzkoa comprise the Basque Country, an Autonomous Community with Nationality Status, home of the distinctive Basque people and their ancient tongue. Navarra and the Basque Country have a unique position within Spain; by giving up their status as kingdoms they received much greater autonomy in what is known as the 'régimen foral'.

The topography of Navarra is a subject which could fill many volumes, its diversity has been categorized into nine main ecosystems divided into three biogeographic areas: the Alpine, the Atlantic and the Mediterranean. Wildlife abounds, accounting for 60 per cent of all species present in Spain – Brown Bears and Bearded Vultures are two of the more unusual creatures. Navarra specializes in rural tourism and, with the establishment of centres in the Roncal and Salazar valleys in 1991, was one of the pioneers of this type of tourism in Spain. Now there are over 800 guest-houses with many awarded the 'Q' for Tourist Quality. They are a great way to get to know the people and their customs.

Bilbao

Below: Bilbao, capital of the Basque Country, houses the Guggenheim Museum. Designed by Frank Gehry, the museum of modern and contemporary art is audacious and striking, earning it the reputation as one of the world's most spectacular buildings.

Navarra

Top: The village of Isaba, in the Roncal Valley.

Above: Two of the main pilgrim routes on the Way of St James cross Navarra, one from the Pyrenees, called the 'French Path' and the other from Aragón. The medieval bridge of La Magdalena is the main entrance for pilgrims into Pamplona from the French Path. Notice the blue sign indicating direction.

Left: The cathedral is on the site of the old Roman city called Pompaelo. It is built in the Gothic style of the 14th and 15th centuries with a neoclassical façade designed by the Spanish architect Ventura Rodríguez. The highlight of the cathedral is the cloister, a masterpiece of Gothic styling.

Right: Leyre Monastery, burnt by the Muslims in the 10th century and rebuilt in 1020, is one of the most important and oldest monastic complexes in Spain. Constructed mainly in the Romanesque style with Gothic additions, it is set in a beautiful landscape. Over the centuries it has been shelter for kings and bishops; it is a place full of legends and myths. Saint Virila, an incumbent abbot apparently went into raptures over the song of the nightingale causing him to sleep for 300 years. Upon waking he made his way back to the monastery where his prolonged slumber was hailed as a miracle. Just to hear the Gregorian chant of the monks certainly justifies the 50-km (31-m) trip from Pamplona.

Below: The Bardenas Reales is a semi-desert, natural park of 42,500 ha (105,020 acres) in the south-east of Navarra. The landscape is amazing and is popular for walking, biking and horseriding.

Opposite below: Over the centuries wood has been an important economic source for the valleys of the Pyrenees. The traditional way of transporting the timber to the Ebro river involved making rafts known as 'almadía' from the tree trunks, equipped with oars to help navigate the dangerous, fast-flowing waters. Every spring a festival is held to celebrate these erstwhile timber transporters on the River Esca. Thousands of spectators watch the logs being manipulated while enjoying the local cuisine; the event culminates with folk-dancing and song.

Catalonia and Barcelona

Capital of Catalonia and second in size only to Madrid, Barcelona boasts that it is the most European town in Spain being only 90 km (56 miles) south of the French border. There are at least two suggestions as to the origins of Barcelona. The mythological Hercules is credited by some as being the founder, if so it appears he was a habitual 'city founder' as several other towns are also attributed to him (see page 68). A more reasonable option involves the Carthaginian general Hamilcar Barca, who probably founded the city in the 3rd century BC. Whoever it was, Barcelona has a rich and fascinating history. No talk of Barcelona would be complete without mentioning the architect Antoni Gaudí, the principal practitioner of Catalan Modernism. Barcelona is Spain's number one tourist destination, which is to be expected considering the architecture, cuisine and culture to be found there.

Above right: The monument to 'Colón' or Christopher Columbus, built for the 1888 Universal Exposition of Barcelona, stands 60 m (197 ft) high. Columbus, according to some, is pointing out to sea, others say he is pointing to the Americas, if so he is pointing in completely the wrong direction.

Right: Bisbe Street, probably the most photographed in Barcelona's Gothic Quarter. The bridge was built in 1928 connecting the Palace of La Generalitat (right, the Gothic façade dates from 1418) to the Casa dels Canonges, which dates from the 14th century.

Above: Las Ramblas is the most famous and liveliest street in the city. It connects Cataluña Square with the Columbus monument. Flower stalls, caged birds and newspapers, music and street shows, terraces and restaurants; it's all there in the one street. According to tradition, if you want to come back to Barcelona you should drink from the Canaletas fountain (in the first part of the street coming from Cataluña Square). Unfortunately the water isn't all that nice, the locals drink bottled.

Left: One of the terraces of the Born quarter, known for its lively bars, cafés and fashionable shops. In the Middle Ages jousting or 'torneos' took place here. Nearby is the Picasso Museum and the magnificent Gothic church, Santa María del Mar. The Plaza Real, located in the Gothic Quarter and not far from las Ramblas, is also a vibrant place at night with restaurants, bars and late-night clubs under the arcade.

This page: Güell Park is named after the businessman who commissioned his friend Gaudí to build a garden city. Only two buildings were ever constructed and Gaudí himself lived in one from 1906 and 1925 (now the Gaudí House Museum). Opened to the public in 1926 the park demonstrates the extent of Gaudí's imagination when given free rein. Mosaic sculptures are a prominent feature.

Opposite below: Gaudí's buildings, domestic and religious, have become symbols of the city. They have a sheer genius and awe-inspiring audacity. The Casa Milá, known popularly as 'La Pedrera' (the stone quarry), built by Gaudí between 1906 and 1912, initially received criticism and even mockery. Salvador Dalí was one of the first to praise the building and he was soon followed by Le Corbusier and others.

Above: The Cathedral of 'La Sagrada Familia' is the most widely known of Gaudí's works. He took over the project in 1883, one year after it was started by another architect and devoted his life to it. It is still, however, unfinished. The projected completion date is 2026, which will be the centenary of Gaudí's death. The cost of construction is by private donation.

Ávila

Ávila, in the autonomous community of Castile and León, has been referred to as the 'Town of Stones and Saints'. This austere medieval town is the burial place of the Grand Inquisitor, Torquemada, and the birthplace of St Teresa as well as of several prominent politicians of the 20th century. The most obvious feature is the complete Medieval stone wall which surrounds the city. It is in such a wonderful state of preservation you could be forgiven for thinking it was built only yesterday. The old town, that is the part enclosed by the walls, has an area of 31 ha (77 acres) and stands at 1,000 m (3,300 ft) above sea level. The town seems to have retained some of its original austerity. There are tourist shops, bars and restaurants but these are not as obvious as in other towns. Ávila offers a wonderful selection of local food from Castilian soup and beans, and potatoes *a la revolcona* (flavoured with paprika) to the succulent steak 'Avileña-negra Ibérica', and finishing up with *yemas* of Santa Teresa, made from egg yolk and sugar, for those with a sweet tooth. Only 111 km (69 miles) north-west from Madrid, the town is easily accessible by rail or road.

Above: The medieval wall, which is the best preserved in Europe, was built around the second half of the 12th century. It is floodlit at night and is the largest, fully illuminated monument in the world. The wall has a perimeter of 2.5 km (1.6 miles), a thickness of 3 m (10 ft) and an average height of 12 m (39 ft) while boasting 88 towers and 9 gates. Stone blocks for its construction were robbed from the nearby Roman necropolis and some Celtic animal sculptures have been found. Two parts of the walls can be visited (be warned, the steps are steep). Wandering through the streets gives you a sense of the past, you can feel a connection with history, you can almost hear the soldiers at work defending the city from their lofty perches on the granite walls. You can enjoy views of the city from the walls or perhaps just let your imagination travel back in time. And if imagination isn't enough, you can be photographed with one of the many street performers dressed in medieval clothes.

Opposite: Built as both temple and fortress, the Cathedral of El Salvador is considered the oldest Gothic cathedral in Spain. Work started in the 9th century, and it took over 300 years to complete. The retroquire (centre) is an excellent example of Renaissance art depicting seven scenes from Christ's childhood.

Segovia

Segovia is probably best known for its fairy-tale castle and Roman aqueduct. Both are wonderfully preserved but the history of the town is one of ups and downs, of kings and revolts. In the 9th century Segovia was under siege, as a civil war raged between Muslim factions and the Christian town was subjected to attacks. The situation was so insecure that tax exemptions and 'fueros' (a form of local constitution) were given as an incentive for people to live there, an unknown system in European feudalism. Segovia's halcyon days were during the 15th century but declined after the terrible plague of 1598. Segovia is 91 km (57 miles) north-west of Madrid by road but travelling by the AVE high-speed train from Madrid's Chamartin station, it is only about a 30-minute journey.

Right: The Alcazar was first a fortress, later a royal palace, then a state prison and now a military academy and archive. The first documentary evidence of it dates from Alfonso VIII (1252–1258) when he and his wife, Leonor the Plantagenet, established their court here. Alfonso X 'El Sabio' (the Wise), who used one of the towers as an astronomical observatory, spent long periods here, while Isabel la Católica came from the Alcazar to be proclaimed queen. One of the many interviews between Isabel and Christopher Columbus took place in the Castle. The Alcazar is reminiscent of a fairy-tale castle and is said to be the inspiration for Walt Disney's portrayal of Cinderella's castle.

Salamanca

Left: Salamanca's late Gothic and Baroque 'New Cathedral' built between the 16th and 18th centuries with the Puente Enrique Estevan in the foreground.

Opposite top: The aqueduct of Segovia, probably dating from the end of the 1st or the beginning of the 2nd century, is one of the best and most complete aqueducts remaining from the Roman Empire. It brings water from the Frío River some 18 km (11 miles) away. Constructed from 20400 granite blocks hewn from the Sierra de Guadarrama and with 166 arches, it is incredible to think that it was built without the use of mortar. Of any kind.

Opposite below: A view of the Cathedral from the Plaza Mayor. This building dates from 1525 after the old cathedral had been destroyed during the revolt of 'Las Comunidades' (1520–1521), a rebellion of the lower order of Castillian aristocracy against the emperor Carlos V. Citizens, tradesmen and the council put up the money for the construction in late-Gothic style during a period when the renaissance style predominated in Spain and Europe.

Chapter 3: Central and Western Spain

Madrid, is the vibrant heart of a vibrant country. Its people, *los Madrileños*, never seem to sleep but inhabit the ubiquitous *terrazas* and *plazas* until the very early hours. In the surrounding region, walled and fortified towns abound. Ancient windmills share hilltops with elegant wind-turbines as the plains stretch south and west into enigmatic Extremadura. This underpopulated region which rubs against the Portuguese border is one of unspoilt nature and well-preserved archaeological remains. The Romans invested heavily in its parched earth leaving arenas and theatres as their legacy.

Below and opposite bottom: The Roman Theatre at Mérida was constructed during the 15th and 16th centuries BC and continued in use for over 300 years. The gods Pluto and Proserpina adorn the façade, while the stand can accommodate 6,000 spectators. The International Festival of Classic Theatre has taken place here every summer since 1933.

Extremadura

Mérida

Extremadura is an autonomous community of western Spain, bordering Portugal. It is an area frequently missed by tourists, but its sparse population makes it ideal for nature lovers and the Monfragüe Natural Park is an unspoilt expanse teaming with wildlife. The capital Mérida isn't on the high-speed rail link and the journey from Madrid by train will take about five hours to cover the 350 km (217 miles) or by road about four hours. Mérida has more Roman monuments than anywhere else in Spain and the 'Archaeological Ensemble of Mérida' was declared a UNESCO World Heritage Site in 1993. Cáceres, 75 km (47 miles) south of Mérida, by contrast is rich in medieval architecture and still has its ancient walls. One remarkable aspect of Cáceres is its population of storks or *cigüeñas*, which build their huge nests on every available platform and can be seen silhouetted against the sky at sunset. Trujillo, 88 km (55 miles) north of Mérida, is another singular town being home to many of Spain's conquistadors, who built grand palaces on their return from the Americas. The number of grand residences weighed against the size of the town is quite amazing.

Right: Mérida's Roman Bridge is 792 m (2,600 ft) long and 12 m (39 ft) above the River Guadiana. Changes in the river and modifications have left little of the original structure. Since 1993, when the Lusitania Bridge (in the background) opened for cars, this bridge has been 'pedestrian only'.

Left: Known as 'Acueducto de los Milagros' (Aqueduct of Miracles), the structure was built around the end of 1st century to bring water from Proserpina Reservoir. It is over 830 m (2,720 ft) long and 25 m (82 ft) at its highest point.

Cáceres

This page: The Plaza Mayor in Cáceres, dating from the 14th century, has multiple uses, as a market, bullring, for Easter celebrations and as a traditional meeting point for the locals. Tournaments were once staged here as well as military parades. You can dine on the delicious Extremaduran cuisine or just have a drink; it is vibrant and exhilarating either by day or by night.

Left: The 11th-century 'Torre del Bujaco' where 40 members of the military and religious order who defended the city during the almohad siege of 1173 were killed by Abu Ya'Qub. The adjacent church is the 'Ermita de la Paz', originally a hermitage but rebuilt in the 18th century.

Below left: The Palace of Los Golfines (15th–16th century) is the biggest palace in the old town. Its beautiful façade groups together three artistic styles, Gothic, Renaissance and Plateresque. The detail shows the Plateresque crenellations with their fantastic animals and the Gothic window displaying the coat-of-arms of the Catholic Kings.

Below: This 'aljibe' (an Arabic word meaning cistern or well), dates from the 11th or 12th century. The subterranean vault collected rainwater and was a vital part of the infrastructure for the military fortress of Cáceres; it now forms part of the city's museum.

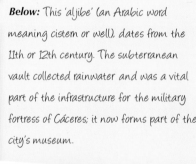

Trujillo

Above: In the 14th century, the Plaza Mayor was simply a church and a market, however when the town was at its peak in the 16th century, it took the form we see today.

Opposite top left: The Palace of Los Pizarro was the home of a brother and daughter of Francisco Pizarro, conqueror of Peru. Built in 1560, it has many remarkable features including a corner balcony surmounted by Pizarro's coat-of-arms, which is itself surrounded by a depiction of the walls of Cuzco (capital of the Inca Empire).

Opposite top right: The Julia Tower of the church of Santa María la Mayor is one of the few remaining Romanesque-style buildings in Extremadura. Construction began in the 14th century over the remains of an earlier Church. It was seriously damaged in the Lisbon earthquake of 1521 but fully restored in the 20th century. The altar screen is painted in Castilian, Flemish and Germanic styles and funerary chapels for the nobility make this the most important religious building in Trujillo.

Opposite below: Built in 1541, the Palace of Juan Pizarro de Orellana, one of the principal figures from the conquest of the Inca Empire, was the first of the grand Renaissance buildings constructed in Trujillo. Miguel de Cervantes stayed here in 1582 as a guest of Fernando Pizarro de Orellana after returning from Portugal.

Madrid

Madrid is one of the most welcoming cities in the world. It has been said that 'If you are in Madrid, you are from Madrid'. However, it has not always been the bustling, lively city that it is today; in the 9th century it was a relatively unimportant backwater. It was Philip II who breathed new life into Madrid by making it the capital of Spain; some say he invented Madrid. Interestingly, one of the worthy king's reasons for choosing Madrid was the lack of aristocracy, thus reducing the potential for conflict. Madrid became the pre-eminent Spanish city overtaking Segovia, Toledo and Salamanca in importance. The architecture of Madrid is subtle, you have to scratch the surface of the city, then you start to discover its wonders. Apart from being superb examples of their respective styles, the buildings are in daily use, so the architecture is an integral part of everyday life for the Madrileños, in harmony with the people. It helps to make the city such a vibrant place. No matter what the season, winter or summer, the nightlife of Madrid has won the city the epithet of 'European capital of the night'. There are places for all tastes. People like to drink in one place for a while, then go on to another and then another, spending all night until breakfast-time 'terrace hopping' and finally finishing up with *churros* and a cup of coffee.

Above: *Located in La Puerta del Sol – a must for any visitor, for shopping, people watching or just drinking a cool beer – the bear is the emblem of the City of Madrid. The bear, which represents Alfonso XI, who used to hunt the animal in the hills near the capital, is eating from the strawberry tree, once plentiful on the outskirts during the Middle Ages.*

Above: One of the most representative monuments of the city, the Puerta de Alcalá opened in 1778 after King Carlos III (known as 'the best Mayor of Madrid') ordered the old brick gate to be demolished. One of the five original gates to the city, it takes its name from the road to Alcalá de Henares on which it is situated.

Opposite right: This famous street, now called the Gran Vía, has changed its name several times. It was conceived in the middle of the 19th century but work didn't start until 1910 due to opposition from residents and shopkeepers as more than 300 houses had to be demolished. The three stretches were eventually finished in 1932. Shown here is a view of the third stretch, from the Plaza Callao to the Plaza de España. On the left is the Carrión building (1931-1933), one of the emblematic buildings of the street. The Hotel Florida once stood here, where war correspondents such as Hemingway, Capa and Taro stayed during the Spanish Civil War. It is good for shopping but the Calle Preciados, near the Puerta del Sol is more important (per square metre it is the most expensive land of the city), also the Calle Serrano, known as the 'golden mile', is home to expensive and international shops.

Above: The Rastro has been a market place for about 500 years. In the middle of the 17th century there were shoemakers, clothes and candle shops here, but by the end of the 18th it had expanded to include the sale of food, trinkets and even objects of questionable provenance. The stalls are open from 09.00 to 15.00 every Sunday and public holidays. The Rastro is the cultural heritage of the people of Madrid and the council doesn't have to the power to close or even alter the market. About 100,000 people visit the market on Sundays, to buy, haggle or simply take in the atmosphere over a glass of wine and tapas before moving on to take lunch.

Above: The Plaza Mayor is located in the heart of the 'Madrid de los Austrias' or the old centre, near the Puerta del Sol. At the beginning of the 17th century the buildings were renovated to give the square a more harmonious look. It has been the setting for popular festivals, bullfighting and coronations since the second decade of the 20th century. Every Sunday there is a market selling stamps and coins, and in December the square is wonderfully adorned with Christmas decorations. For a snack, a calamari sandwich, so typical of Madrid, is recommended.

Right: The Museo del Prado is one of the most important art galleries in the world. The building was designed by Juan de Villanueva and was to be the centre for natural sciences after the modernization of the city by Carlos III. His grandson, Fernando VII designated the building as a museum on the advice of his wife María Isabel and it was opened to the public in 1819. The paintings are from royal collections beginning with those of Carlos V in the 16th century. It is especially abundant with European masters from the 16th to the 19th century, including, to name only a few, Velázquez, El Greco, Goya, Titian, Rubens and El Bosco.

Left: The Royal Palace was built between 1738 and 1764 after its magnificent predecessor was destroyed by a Christmas Eve fire in 1734, and continued as a royal residence until 1931. The west façade looks out onto the 'Campo del Moro' park. To complete the park, as envisaged by Philip II, took three centuries mainly due to the steep terrain and shortages of water and cash. Opened to the public in 1978, its beautiful and peaceful 20 ha (49 acres) are an ideal place to relax after a visit to the palace.

Below left: Retiro Park is a favourite place for locals and visitors alike in which to enjoy walking, sitting on a shady terrace, skating or just playing with the children. Covering more than 125 ha (309 acres), it includes gardens, two palaces for exhibitions, fountains and sculptures, with the 'Fallen Angel' sculpture being the only one in the world dedicated to Satan. Begun in the 17th century, it was originally for the exclusive use of royalty. Many plays by, among others, Lope de Vega and Calderón de la Barca, were enacted here. In the 18th century ordinary citizens were allowed access.

Right: According to the Guinness Book of Records, the Casa Botín is the oldest restaurant in the world. It's a place to enjoy traditional Spanish food, especially the suckling pig and lamb roasted in an oven that has seen service since the restaurant was opened in 1725. The writers Pérez Galdós, Pío Baroja, Hemingway and Graham Greene have been among its clients. Madrid offers many kinds of restaurants, from the expensive to the low cost, traditional or avant-gardist, with Spanish or international cuisine.

Castille La Mancha and Toledo

Toledo is known as the 'City of Three Cultures' because of the pacific coexistence there of Christians, Jews and Muslims. It was the capital of the Spanish Empire until the middle of the 16th century. The narrow cobbled streets lead this way and that, opening onto small squares and enchanting buildings, churches, monasteries and wonderfully preserved dwellings. Tourism is the main industry and visitor numbers are high. Festivals such as Corpus Christi and the Semana Santa attract such numbers that the city becomes suffocated with humanity but the atmosphere and ambiance created is well worth putting up with the crush of bodies and packed terraces. It was designated a UNESCO Heritage Site in 1986, which will guarantee the preservation of this remarkable city.

Left: The 'Street of the Angel' is one of the narrow streets of the Jewish quarter. Some historians calculate over 12,000 Jews lived in the city during 12th century. They were forcibly moved to the Jewish quarter in 1480 on the order of the Catholic Kings in the Cortes of Toledo.

Opposite top: The Museum of El Greco exhibits the painter's work and also that of others in a recreation of a contemporary house. El Greco was born in Crete but came to Toledo in 1577 where he lived until his death in 1614.

Opposite below: Toledo sits on a horseshoe-shaped bend of the River Tajo, 70 km (43 miles) south of Madrid. The elevation of the old town is somewhat higher than the surrounding area giving it the impression of being an island, although to the north it is accessible without the need of a bridge. The city is dominated by the Alcázar. Rebuilt after the Spanish Civil war, it now houses the Castilla-La Mancha Regional Library ('Biblioteca Autonómica') and the Army Museum ('Museo del Ejército').

Valencia

Right: Third largest after Madrid and Barcelona, Valencia has had millions spent on its tourist infrastructure in recent years. The 'Ciudad de las Artes y las Ciencias' (City of Arts and Sciences) is evidence of this (pictured). The 'Lonja de la Seda', a gothic civil building, is UNESCO listed and. 'Los Jardines del Turia' is a 9-km (5½-mile) garden which crosses the city, good for biking, walking or a trip on the tourist train.

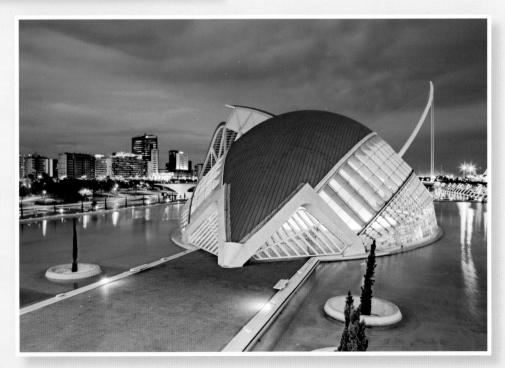

Chapter 4: Southern and Eastern Spain

The coastal plains of southern and eastern Spain are home to the many costas so familiar with tourists from northern Europe. Andalucía is Spain's most southerly region. Its sun-drenched beaches have given many their first taste of Spain, whetting appetites for travel further afield. Inland, the southern slopes of the Sierra Nevada shelter the unspoilt villages of La Alpujarra. The historic city of Córdoba is remarkable in its splendour, while Seville is truly Andalucían in every sense. Deserts and cave houses, mountain ranges and fertile plains all conspire to produce an area of amazing contrast, a summer playground and cultural classroom that is essentially Spanish.

Below: Málaga has 14 km (8½ miles) of beaches, and many restaurants where the specialities of the city can be sampled, such as 'pescaíto frito' (small fried fish) and the 'espetos de sardine' (sardines grilled over charcoal).

Málaga

Málaga with almost 3,000 years of history is one of the world's oldest cities. It is a city of culture, art and architecture on the popular Costa del Sol. Home of Pablo Picasso, the Picasso Museum was opened in 2003 according to his desire to have a museum in his home town. It contains 233 works, covering the period from 1892 to 1972. The house where he was born is also open to visitors. Those interested in art can also visit the Pompidou Centre, the first outside Paris. Opened in 2013, it exhibits works from 20th and 21st centuries by artists such as Francis Bacon, Max Ernst, Magritte and Frida Kahlo.

Other attractions are the cathedral (17th–18th century), the Roman theatre (1st century) and the castle of Gibralfaro (14th century) with its impressive views of the city. The English cemetery was the first Protestant cemetery to be built in Spain (19th century).

Almería

Almería is no stranger to mishap having suffered at least four major earthquakes and being destroyed by the especially violent quake of 1522. During the Spanish Civil War (1936–1939), the town was severely bombed by the German Condor Legion, which was deliberately targeting refugees who had taken shelter there after fleeing Málaga in 1937. Nowadays the town and province in general have blossomed into an affluent and important area of Spain, due to tourism and the fruit and vegetable industry. Produce destined for the markets of northern Europe grow in acres of plastic tunnels that cover the landscape. Although this is an arid area, it is made fertile with adequate irrigation.

Below: *Vélez Blanco is the location of the neolithic Los Letreros cave. A painting of either a human figure with a bow or a god holding a rainbow was discovered there in 1868, named the 'Indalo Man'. It reputedly brings good luck and many items depicting the symbol are available in tourist shops. No refunds are available, however, if the Indalo Man fails to perform. The castle overlooking the town dates from the 16th century.*

Cabo de Gata

The Cabo de Gata Natural Park in the south-eastern corner of Andalucía is the first and largest protected area in the region. It's a place of dramatic secluded beaches, hidden coves and coral reefs; 100-m (328-ft) high cliffs fall steeply into the clear blue Mediterranean. Inland, the prospect is no less dramatic with the eponymous mountain boasting Spain's largest volcanic rock formation. Covering a terrestrial area of 45,663 ha (112,836 acres) and with a protected marine zone of 12,200 ha (30,147 acres), it was designated a UNESCO Biosphere Reserve in 1997. Despite its arid climate there are more than 1,000 plant species in this Natural Park, including the prickly pear.

Above and centre: The Cabo de Gata Natural Park has over 50 km (31 miles) of coastal cliffs, which are the best preserved in the European Mediterranean. The southernmost point is at 'Las Sirenas' (The Mermaids), so-called because of the evocative rock formations jutting out of the sea (above). 'Los Genoveses' beach (left) is typical of the long, wild beaches and hidden coves that alternate along the coast.

Left: This waterwheel in the small village of Pozo de los Frailes was built at the beginning of the 20th century and remained in use until 1983. This device shows the importance of finding underground water, as the volcanic Sierra de Cabo de Gata lacks rivers and only has 195 mm (8 in) of rain per year.

Tabernas

This page: *The Tabernas Desert (right) in Almería province, approximately 60 km (37 miles) from the Cabo de Gata, is the driest region of Europe and has the continent's only true desert climate with less than 200 mm (8 in) of rain per year. It is a protected natural park covering an area of 280 sq km (110 sq miles). The landscape is dramatic and arid, having an average yearly temperature of almost 18°C (64°F) in the low-lying areas.*

The Tabernas Desert was the location for over 300 films including the genre of 'Spaghetti Westerns'. Almería was known as the European Hollywood during the 1960s and 70s. With so many different languages being spoken, the shooting of these co-productions could become quite chaotic. Clint Eastwood, who appeared in many of these, described the sets as 'Towers of Babel'. Many former film sets have been turned into popular theme parks attracting foreign and domestic tourists (below right).

Granada

Few cities in the world can compare to the sheer beauty of Granada. The last Muslim stronghold to be taken by Ferdinand and Isabella in their 'Christian Reconquest', it still retains an Arabic ambience. There are several Arab baths where you can relax and rejuvenate after a busy day sightseeing. Drenched in sun and overlooked by the magnificent Alhambra complex, its streets are a joy to stroll through.

The steep northern face of the Sierra Nevada is in contrast to the gentle rolling southern slopes, where a unique area of Spain called La Alpujarra enjoys a micro-climate as curious as its people. Singular geological conditions to the east of the province in the Guadix area theoretically allow one to build a climatically controlled home with nothing more than a shovel. When the earth is initially exposed, it is pliable and can be dug easily, after exposure it hardens over time making this an ideal place for the digging of caves.

Above: A view of the Albaicín quarter (a UNESCO World Heritage Site) from the Alhambra, both inhabited by Muslims in 756. Be sure to take a walk in its narrow streets or just sit in one of its many squares enjoying the beautiful views of the Alhambra, especially at sunset.

Left: Originally from the Arab period, the 'carmen' (meaning 'vineyard' in Arabic) is the traditional type of dwelling in Granada, consisting of a house, garden and orchard, all surrounded by high masonry walls. The sloping gardens are built as terraces and consist of fruits, trees for shade, flowers, vegetables and box hedges. The most sought-after are in the Albaicín area because of the wonderful views. Pictured is the 'Carmen de la Victoria', property of the university of Granada. The gardens are maintained as they were 100 years ago.

The Alhambra

Above: The Alhambra (meaning 'red fortress' in Arabic) is by far the best example of the splendour reached by Nasrid art. The complex consists of the Alcazaba or fortress (right) and the Royal Palace (left). The Alcazaba is the oldest part of the Alhambra, started in 1239.

Right: The Generalife villa was built around the middle of the 13th century in 'El Cerro del Sol' (Hill of the Sun). It was conceived as a rural villa, with orchards and gardens. Water in the Generalife and the Nasrid Palaces was designed as an omnipresent element, not only for irrigation but also as an aesthetic motif playing with reflections and light. Sound from the constantly moving water contributes to relaxation while the garden's scent adds another sensory element.

Right and below right: The 'Patio de los Leones' in the palace of the same name was built in the middle of the 14th century. Its structure is typical of Muslim Spain with open-air courtyards surrounded by room spaces. The courtyard was reopened in 2012 after restoration work on the 12 lions, which took ten years.

Below: The 'Cuarto Dorado' or 'Golden Room' got its name from its beautiful ceiling.

La Alpujarra

Above: In La Alpujarra, as in all Andalucía, people take great pride in their floral displays on house walls and in patios. Typically the villages of La Alpujarra have very narrow and steep streets. It can be exhausting but worthwhile exploring these enchanting pueblos.

Above right: The village of Órgiva in the south of the region with its twin church towers.

Guadix

Right: Guadix in Granada province has the largest number of cave dwellings in Spain. Considered in the past as substandard housing, they are now regarded as important bioclimatic homes by maintaining a temperature of between 15 and 19°C (59–66°F) where outside temperatures can vary between 0 and 40°C (32–104°F). There are many hotels and apartments in the area where the curious can experience this type of dwelling.

Seville

Seville is the capital of Andalucía and the largest town in southern Spain. According to legend, it was founded by Hercules and was an integral part of the ancient Tartessian civilization. Seville today is known for its sparkle and joy of life with a vitality which enchants the visitor. Carmen, Figaro and Don Juan are all evocative of the Sevillian character, all larger than life, which is the impression one gets from the city's monumental architecture. If the wonderful parks and gardens are the 'lungs' of Seville then one must not forget the 'stomach', gazpacho soup and fried seafood is a delightful combination.

Below: The Catedral de Santa María is the largest Catholic cathedral in the world. It is said that when the council took the decision in the 14th century to construct a new civic building, one particularly conscientious priest remarked: "Let's build a temple of such a size that everybody will believe us to be insane". Work continued up until the 19th century with renovations and additions, however the main influences are Gothic, Renaissance and Baroque.

To the left is the façade of the Archivo General de Indias built in the 16th century by the eminent architect Juan de Herrera originally as a market. Since the 18th century it has been used as an archive for administrative documents relating to Spain's colonial past. About 40,000 individual files, over 8,000 maps and 80 million written pages are housed there. Both the cathedral and archive have been UNESCO World Heritage Sites since 1987.

Above: The Plaza de España in María Luisa Park covers more than 50,000 sq m (538,196 sq ft). It was built for the 1929 Exposición Iberoamericana with work starting in 1914. One of the most spectacular examples of the regionalist style, its semi-elliptical shape symbolizes Spain's embrace of its old colonies. The structure has appeared in the films 'Lawrence of Arabia' and 'The Wind and the Lion', as well as 'Star Wars II' (as a digitally modified image). Built into it are remarkable, tiled recesses depicting every Spanish province (see page 10).

Right: The 12th-century Puerta del León leads to the Reales Alcázares, the oldest continuously occupied royal palace in the world.

Above: The Torre del Oro or Golden Tower got its name from its gold hue produced by the mortar, lime and pressed straw from which it is constructed. The first level was built in the 13th century by the Almohade governor of Seville, the second by the Peter I in the 14th century and the third in 1769. It is one of the most symbolic buildings of the city.

Right: Plaza Jesús de la Pasión has been a centre of commercial activity since the 14th century. The outstanding building of the Plaza is Pedro Roldán', built in 1925 and designed by José Espiau Muñoz. The style is known as 'regionalist' (from the first third of the 20th century), featuring a combination of brick, tiles, large windows and ornamental grilles.

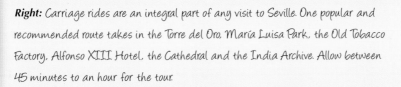

Above: The Metropol Parasol, known popularly as 'La Seta de la Encarnación' (Incarnation's Mushroom) was designed by the German architect, Jurgen Mayer, and inaugurated in 2012. Contained within the Parasol are shops, restaurants and panoramic terraces, while the underground level houses the Antiquarium, where important Roman remains discovered on the site are displayed.

Right: Carriage rides are an integral part of any visit to Seville. One popular and recommended route takes in the Torre del Oro, María Luisa Park, the Old Tobacco Factory, Alfonso XIII Hotel, the Cathedral and the India Archive. Allow between 45 minutes to an hour for the tour.

Córdoba

Córdoba in Andalucía has been a favoured site for human habitation since earliest times, Neanderthal remains found in the area date back at least 40,000 years. However, it was under Muslim rule that the city flourished. The Great Mosque is a reminder of the glory days of Córdoba and should be on every visitor's list. The city is well within reach of Madrid being on the AVE high-speed train link – it takes just under two hours to complete the 400-km (250-mile) journey. One word of warning: be prepared for heat, as it has the highest average summer daily temperatures in Europe averaging 36.9°C (98°F) in July and August. Córdoba is unique in its culture and racial tolerance. During the 10th century its fame spread to the far reaches of northern Europe prompting the Saxon nun, Hroswitha, a poet and dramatist, to call the city 'The Ornament of the World'.

Below: A view of Córdoba from the 'Alcazar of the Christian Kings'. Capital of Hispania Ulterior during the Roman Period, it was captured by Islamic armies in 711, then declared an Independent Caliphate of Damascus in 929 by Abderramán III. From 929 to 976 Córdoba reached its pinnacle of splendour. It was the most important city of Europe culturally, in the scientific field and economically; its population exceeded 500,000. It boasted 3,000 mosques, 300 public baths and a library with possibly a million books. By the end of the 10th century most of the books had been either burnt or sold and the prestige of the city waned during the infighting between the various Muslim factions.

Left: *The Alcazar of the Christian Kings was once part of the Caliph's Palace. It has served many needs: royal residence, seat of the Spanish Inquisition and even a jail in the 19th century.*

Below: *A view from Calahorra Tower of the Roman Bridge (or 'Old Bridge' as it is known locally) spanning the Guadalquivir River. The bridge has been in use for 2,000 years and was the only bridge serving Córdoba until 1953 when the Puente de San Rafael was inaugurated.*

Above: The oldest part of the Great Mosque of Córdoba, built by Abderrarraman I (785). Roman and Visigothic shafts and capitals were reused to give the impression of a forest of columns. Each one of the eleven naves had its own gate leading to the Patio de los Naranjos, but most of them were blocked off when the mosque was converted into a Christian temple. In the 16th century a cathedral was built in the middle of the Mosque. King Carlos I said, when he saw the finished result, "You have destroyed what was not found anywhere by building something that can be found everywhere".

Left: The original minaret of the Great Mosque was built by Abd al-Rahmán III but was used as a Christian bell tower in the 14th century. The tower has been plagued by natural disasters, however, damaged by a storm in 1589 and not restored until 1617, only to be hit by another storm. Then in 1755 the Lisbon earthquake caused such devastation to the tower that it took eight years to rebuild.

Left: The statue of Rabí ibn Maymón (1138-1204), known as 'Maimónides'. Córdoba was the birthplace of three important philosophers: the Roman Séneca, the Muslim Averroes and his disciple, the Jewish Maimónides. Maimónides' studies in Rabbinic science, language and culture were interrupted in 1148 when the city fell under the religious fanaticism of the Almohades. In 1160 he moved to Fez with his family and then to Egypt, where he lived for most of his life, working as a highly respected doctor. He is regarded as the preeminent Jewish thinker of the Middle Ages.

Left: The Medina Azahara or 'Bright City', is eight kilometres (five miles) west of Córdoba. Abd al-Rahmán III ordered its building in 936 as his seat of the government. He spared no expense with some 10,000 men working on its construction, and with rich purple and red marble, gold and precious stones incorporated into the structure. It took over 25 years to build but was destroyed only 75 years later during infighting. Only the façade of the House of Ya'far at Medina Azahara remains. It was once the residence of the city's prime ministers.

Getting About

The airports at Madrid, Barcelona and Málaga are well served by international airlines and low-cost airlines connect most of Spain's major cities offering the usual benefits of air travel. Barcelona and Málaga are also popular destinations for cruise ships, as is Cádiz.

Getting around in Spain is made easy by a modern integrated transport system. Renfe Operadora is the train service provider that operates on the ADIF infrastructure with more than 15,000 km (9,300 miles) of track, both are state owned. Renfe's long-distance 'AVE' service is the high-speed train network that connects Madrid, Barcelona and the main cities of the south and east. It touches speeds of 300 kph (186 mph) with the 540-km (336-mile) journey from Madrid to Seville taking just two and a half hours. The trains are clean, quiet and seem to glide on the rails. On longer journeys videos are shown with complimentary ear-phones supplied.

The 'slow trains' are as well turned out as the AVE and some journeys are a sheer delight as well as inexpensive. The journey on the slow train from Madrid´s Chamartín station to Segovia, a distance of some 100 km (62 miles), takes two

hours and travels over the Sierra de Guadarrama through picturesque mountain villages and breathtaking landscape. Segovia is on the AVE route but uses a tunnel under the Sierra. Toledo, to the south of Madrid, is also serviced by the AVE.

If booking a train ticket in Madrid, then book online whenever possible or at one of the smaller stations. If you have no option but to use the booking office at Madrid's main Atocha station, then take a survival pack with you, as it is almost always crowded with waits of up to several hours.

Coach travel is another viable option with buses radiating out from Madrid to all parts of Spain. The main coach station, Estacion Sur, is part of the massive Méndez Álvaro hub with connections to the Metro, Renfe services and the local bus network, while the Estación de Avenida de América serves destinations to the north of Madrid. The coaches are modern, air-conditioned and like all public transport in Spain, punctual.

For travel within Madrid the Metro is recommended. With almost 300 km (186 miles) of track and over 300 stations, it is one of the largest networks in Europe. Fares are reasonable and it is possible to buy a 'Metrobus' ticket, which can be used for ten journeys on the local bus or Metro. The Metro operates from 06:05 until 02:00 seven days a week. The local bus service is efficient and low-cost, enabling visitors to sightsee, but traffic snarl-ups can be a problem.

Opposite: Taking a train from Atocha Station is a wonderful experience. The old arched station has been turned into a tropical garden with about 400 plants from the Americas, Asia and Australia.

Above: The traffic-free dual carriageway leading to Condado de Alhama, Murcia province.

Resources

TRANSPORT

Getting about mainland Spain is made easy by the use of technology, online booking, e-tickets, etc.

Train

When booking a journey on the state-run railway system, it is advisable to do it online to avoid language misunderstandings. Some towns have stations solely for the AVE (high-speed train), so when searching on the RENFE site, make sure all stations at a given location are selected. Bookings can be made at www.renfe.com/EN/viajeros.

Coach

Some coach operators are regional and if you use Madrid as the hub then to the south and the Costa del Sol, Daibus offer regular and low-cost services. The online booking page in English is www.movelia.es/en. For destinations to the east of Madrid the operator is AVANZA at www.avanzabus.com/web/destinations.html. The largest coach operator is ALSA at www.alsa.es/en which covers most of Spain. The main coach station is Méndez Alvaro Transport Interchange & Estación Sur Bus Station at www.estacionautobusesmadrid.com

Metro

The Madrid metro has a website www.metromadrid.es/en.

Airlines

http://www.iberia.com
http://www.iberiaexpress.com
http://www.easyjet.com
https://www.ryanair.com

TOURISTS OFFICES

Toledo tourist office: www.toledo-turismo.com
Madrid tourist office:www.esmadrid.com
Granada tourist office: www.granadatur.com

ACKNOWLEDGEMENTS

The Museo Arqueológico Nacional Madrid for allowing us the unrestricted use of images.
To el Museo de Altamira for the image of the wonderful cave painting.
Santiago de Compostela de Turismo for the hospitality shown to us during our visit.
Also to the Navarra Tourist Board for the many high-quality images they supplied.

ABOUT THE AUTHORS

John MacDonald shares his time between the UK and Spain and has written for many Spanish and international publications. He studied journalism, photography and archaeology at the University of Exeter and UCL, and has a special interest in Spanish history.

Patricia Díaz Pereda studied audiovisual communication and literature at the Complutense University of Madrid and has worked as a television director after studying at the School of Spanish Television. She lives in Madrid and has been published in many literary magazines.

Index

For Celia and Santiago

First published in the United Kingdom in 2016 by John Beaufoy Publishing,
11 Blenheim Court, 316 Woodstock Road, Oxford OX2 7NS, England
www.johnbeaufoy.com

ISBN 978-1-909612-70-9

Designed by Glyn Bridgewater
Cartography by William Smuts
Project management by Rosemary Wilkinson

Printed in Malaysia by Times Offset (M) Sdn Bhd

All photos by John MacDonald except for: Barcelona Tourist Office (p40b, 41b, 42b); National Museum & Research
Centre of Altamira: P Saura (p11t); Navarra Tourist Office (p37, 38, 39); Official Tourist Office of Navarra (p25); Ana
Muela Pareja (p73, 74t, 75t); Patronato de Turismo de la Costa del Sol (p4l); Patricia Díaz Pereda (p20t, 27t, 31t, 32tr, 58t,
59t); Santiago de Compostela Turismo (p30); Shutterstock.com:peresanz (p2), Sean Pavone (p4), patjo (p8br), Joseph Sohm
(p9t), Arena Photo UK (p9b), Vladimir Sazonov (p15b), Kiev.Victor (p16), kapyos (p18t), Matej Kastelic (p23), Darios
(p28), Rainer Herhaus (p29), Santi Rodriguez (p36), Luti (p41t), Vladitto (p42t), 135pixels (p43t), BrunoGarridoMacias
(p45b), guillermo77 (p47b), 2xSamara.com (p59b); Tourist Office Asturias (p7t, 35br); Tourist Office Asturias: Antonio
Vázquez (p3tc, 34b), Eduardo Velasco (p33t), Camilo Alonso (p33b, 34t), José Suárez (p35c, 35bl), Ana Müller (p35t);
Tourist Office of Valencia (p20b); Turisme de Barcelona, Espai d'Imatge (p24b); Turismo Valencia (p24t).

Cover captions and credits

Front cover (top, left to right): *Casa Milá, Barcelona* © John MacDonald; *Bullring, Madrid* © Shutterstock/Tatiana Popova;
Great Mosque of Córdoba © Patricia Díaz Pereda; *Metropol Parasol, Seville* © John MacDonald. Front cover (centre):
Semana Santa, Toledo © Dani Martín. Front cover (bottom): *The Alhambra* © John MacDonald. Back cover (left to right):
The art of damasquinado © Patricia Díaz Pereda; *Feria del Rosario* © John MacDonald; *La Alpujarra* © John MacDonald;
The Golden Tower, Seville © John MacDonald.